11/06

AMERICUS

BOOK I

AMERICUS

BOOK I

BY
LAWRENCE
FERLINGHETTI

A NEW DIRECTIONS BOOK

Book design by Sylvia Frezzolini Severance and Lawrence Ferlinghetti
Cover by the author
Manufactured in the United States of America
New Directions Books are printed on acid-free paper.
First published clothbound by New Directions in 2004
Published simultaneously in Canada by Penguin Books Canada Limited

Library of Congress Cataloging-in-Publication Data

Ferlinghetti, Lawrence.
    Americus / by Lawrence Ferlinghetti.
        p. cm.
    Includes bibliographical references.
    ISBN 0-8112-1578-4 (acid-free paper)
        1. National characteristics, American—Poetry. 2. United States—Poetry.
    I. Title.

PS3511.E557A83 2004
811'.54—dc22

                                2003028142

New Directions Books are published for James Laughlin
by New Directions Publishing Corporation,
80 Eighth Avenue, New York, NY 10011

CONTENTS

I

To summarize the past by theft and allusion
with a parasong a palimpsest
a manuscreed writ over
a graph of consciousness at best
a consciousness of 'felt life'
A rushing together
of the raisins of wrath
of living and dying
the laughter and forgetting
The maze and amaze of life

Sound of the eternal dialogue
echoing through the centuries
of all the voices that ever sang or wrote
(bearers of our consciousness)
And the flux of history
interrupted by catastrophes
Flowers blooming out of season
Sound of weeping beyond reason
A pianist playing in the ruins of Prague
A London fog
A cow a clod at a country crossing
Dark dawn and a rooster's cry *ki-ki-ri-ki!*
A light that ever was on land and sea
and tea at Rumplemeyer's
in the Rue Rivoli
The labyrinth on the floor of Chartres Cathedral
and a Warsaw concerto heard distantly
on a Detroit mall
full of gumball goombahs on rollerskates
Cry of a black singer
in a beat-up Harlem bar
A bat hitting a ball
in the first game of a new season
Laughter in a eucalyptus forest

in a smiling summer dream
and fool's gold gleaming
in a California stream

All the images of
the splendid life of the world
down the rivers of windfall light
A trillion trillion images
kaleidoscopic in a psychedelic tropic
(later boiled down to a seminar topic)
A song resung
by a bird flown over
to another zone another climate

Primate mutated in many colors
Wrought from the dark in his mother long ago
from the dark of ancient Europa
Euro man and Euro woman
in the hold of a listing freighter
with Americus in the womb
born by the Hudson and Grant's Tomb

And he did suffer a sea change
(suffered and did not suffer)
to spring forth upon a new place
a kind of Atlantis lost and found
(athwart a passage to India)
A kind of two-legged creature
An embryonic creation
half-liberated spirit
blithe and tempest-tossed
An unknowing quantity
that could grow into almost anything
in the great unknown
Some kind of new woman or man
dreamed up
in our great smelting pot
petri dish of creation

A small-scale exhibition
of what mankind could possibly be—

"Demon or bird! (said the boy's soul)"
Hero or antihero
Man of pure action or Underground Man
Man of "heightened consciousness"
or psychedelic mystic
Slave master or utopian dreamer
Bowery bohunk or blessed redeemer
Sister of Mercy or serial killer
Poet or panderer on the lamb
Keystone Kop or Chaplin's little man
or Bush League Presidencies
in totalitarian plutocracies?
O which will it be?

America the greatest experiment on earth
with the greatest chance to create
a higher human being
A reconditioned anima or animus
bandy-legged and gender-blended
A cuss upon the cusp
of civilization
White mutt or *mestizo*
at home on the two continents of America
made of many cultures and calamities

Men Seeking Women
Women Seeking Men
Men Seeking Men
Women Seeking Women
Lover Seeking Lover
in search of self or some other
Self-made heroes or antiheroes
Foolscape fool or far-out cat
Have time, will travel—

He the journeyman poet
on the Open Road
He Abe the railsplitter
And Ahab the whaler
And Sinbad the Sailor
And Thoreau at Walden Pond
And young Tom Paine
And John Brown at Harper's Ferry
And Lindbergh in an open car
in a Fifth Avenue parade
And Gentleman Gene Tunney and Babe Ruth and Jackie Robinson
And Gertrude Stein making Americans
(in her own image)
And Gatsby kissing Daisy on a sailboat in the Sound
And Studs Lonigan and Studs Terkel
And Thorstein Veblen
(who drank the bitter drink all right)
And Carl Sandburg and Vachel Lindsay
beating on a barrel with the handle of a broom
And young Thomas Wolfe
(his green hero Eugene)
riding across the dark land
(ghost of Stephen Dedalus)
alone on a train in the deep South
And Ti-Jean Kerouac at Columbia
dreaming of Mexico *Under the Volcano*
And Tom and Huck and Jim
on the great river late and soon—

He was an American
He was an American boy
He read the *American Boy* magazine
and became a Boy Scout
in the suburbs
He thought he was Tom Sawyer
catching crayfish in the Bronx River
and imagining the Mississippi
He had a baseball mitt

and an American Flyer bike
He delivered the *Woman's Home Companion*
at five in the afternoon
or the *Herald Trib*
at five in the morning

It was long since he was a herdsman

II

So that—Beginning with Sunday at the beach
                              or some other *jubilatus*
                                        of life on earth
              An antic vision of a beach somewhere
                  Shoals of bodies lying side by side
                      Strands of lovers braided together
                              into love-knots besotted
                                        (or not knotted)
One body one breathing human plasm
One body rolls over
              and a thousand others flip
                      revealing sandy faces
                                  breasts and crotches
                  the nests and roots of humankind
                              (so oft unkind)
                                        Castaways all!

A lighthouse pulsing even at midday
and at midnight sweeping in circles
like time itself
"Time the wisest of things
for it finds out everything"
Time the fourth dimension
An arrow flying both ways
through bent space
The tick of time man-made
And the sun sweeping in cycles
over time zones
lighting up far places and faces
as memory does
beyond sequential time
as in dreams our memories
are selective and surreal
Images fled together in dream
from all parts in time and space
superimposed upon each other

Dadaist collages
flashed upon our mindscreen
the World Trade Center's twin towers
on the Champs Élysées
Aunt Rose's roses pinned upon
a Pocahontas statue by Rodin
Daddy's penis in Dante's hand
as getting and spending
we lay waste our trousers

So with our memory
pillaging the past
to make the present
dreaming through the centuries
trading time for tenses
as the candid-camera-eye-called-mind
blesses and distresses humankind
(the thinkpad making
cowards of us all)

    The great gulls soaring over
                hearing the sea with hidden ears
  A holiday scene again
        A boardwalk again
                Atlantic City or Rockaway
Houses of glass
        Houses of cards
            Cities thrown up
  Rosie rolls her garter up
        The sun shines down forever and forever

                Will the world ever end?

Balancing a box of doughnuts on his head
a cocky kid threads his way
through the late election rally
"Get yer cruellers!" he cries
with vestigial German accent

"This race makes a difference!"
cries the Tammany Hall fat cat
running for mayor
(Sez who? Boss Tweed snorts)
On the Elevated, back of the car
a black woman thinks
"It's dangerous to be born with breasts"
Mother in the street, her brassiere backwards
Life rolling on
and memory a shuttle
between past and present
a shuttered train full of shattered mirrors

> *Don't tell me, don't tell me*
> *What train I'm on*
> *So they can't find me . . .*

III

And Homer came
looking like Odysseus
drifting over oceans and tilled fields
with brittle leaves that whispered as he came
And he spoke up in *alta voce*
in wild demonic
demotic Greek quoth he
with tongue halfway in cheek:

"Walt Whitman your greatest soul speaker
with his 'barbaric yawp'
sounding for the first time
free from the past
the voice of the people of America
at once joyous and tragic
passionate and calm
intimate as a lover
And when you touched his book
you touched himself
And many were Whitman's wild children
following after
(singing—
touching each other)
and many the others who disclaimed him . . .

"Your era lit and littered
with brave attempts at great epics
like old Ezra's *Cantos*—
canti that couldn't possibly be sung—
in which he claimed to have brought us
the great crystal ball
(or Crystal Palace)
The *Cantos* his *Commedia*
a human comedy with little comedy
(lacking the extra dimension

of pure laughter)
a dimmer tragedy than Dante's
with a certain sublimity a certain grandeur
and precious little light
at the end of the tunnel
whereas Dante's *Paradiso*
"the place where all is light"
a place that surely must exist
in the farthest reaches of sky
(as Heinrich Olbers later astronomized)

"And self-exiled Ez
baffled into silence
while the thought of what America would be like
if the *Cantos* had a wider circulation
troubled his sleep

"And then Doc Williams' *Paterson*
its life in its Falls
in which he heard
the plash and eddy
the profane refrain
of American speech
as opposed to gabby British pub-talk
as strained through the ears of Reverend Eliot
or *la langue épuisée* of French existentialists
hung up between Being and Nothingness

"And then Olson's surgent *Maximus*
(a whale of a man was he
dubbing himself Ishmael)
talking to his sea-blown city
O Gloucester
and talking always to himself
(with a certain incoherence)
to tell "who obeys the figures
of the present dance"
A profoundly private mumbling
for all its maxing-out

'in this foul country where
human lives are so much trash'

"And yet—and yet—" great rapper Homer went on—
"Dare I say to you that poetry
ain't what it used to be
since there ain't no Ulysses around to carry tales
Oh lend me your ears lend me your tears
all you finger-poppin' daddies of poetry
gifted with 'giftlessness'
you poet's poets writing poetry about poetry
you deconstructed language poets
you far-out freaked-out cut-up poets
you prestressed Concrete poets
you pay-toilet poets groaning with graffiti
you cunnilingual poets
you A-train swingers who never swing on birches
you eyeless unrealists
you self-occulting supersurrealists
you Nuyorican slammers and gangsta rappers
you bedroom visionaries
and closet agitpropagators
you Groucho Marxist poets
and leisure class comrades
(who sleep 'til noon
and talk about the working-class proletariat)
you poetry workshop poets
you masters of the sawmill haiku
in the boondock heart of America
you lovers of suicided poets
you den mothers of poetry
you Zen brothers of poetry
you hairy professors of poesie
and all you poetry critics
drinking the blood of the poet
all you poetry police—

"Take heed take heed
all you who still should be

the gadflies of the state
Here is my burning answer
to the ever-moldering question
as to what poetry can be
(which I being blind can see
better than thou)—

"Poetry a graph of high consciousness.
Poetry the truth that reveals all lies.
Poetry a camera eye without a shutter
looking down both roads that diverge in a narrow wood.
Words wait to be reborn in the shadow of the lamp of poetry.
The flight path of a poem must be upward or it will crash.
Poems are emails from the unknown, beyond cyberspace.
Poetry as a first language came before writing and still sounds in us,
    a mute music, an inchoate music.
Poetry is white writing on black, black writing on white.
Poems like moths beat against the window trying to reach the light.
It is a madeleine dipped in Proust's tea.
It is a player piano in an abandoned seaside casino, still playing.
Poetry is what we would cry out upon coming to ourselves in a dark
    wood in the middle of the journey of our life.
Poetry is news from the growing edge on the far frontiers of
    consciousness.
Poetry is a mute melody in the head of every dumb animal.
It is a descant rising out of the heart of darkness.
It is the light at the end of the tunnel and the darkness within it.
It is the morning dove mourning night.
It is the morning dove mourning love, and nothing cries out like the
    cry of the heart.
Every great poem fulfills a longing and puts life back together.
Every bird a word, every word a bird, and birdsong is not made by
    machines.
Poetry is boat-tailed birds singing in the setting sun in the tops of
    jacaranda trees on the plaza of San Miguel de Allende.
It is all the birds of the universe flocking together for a congress of
    birds and singing singly.
And every poem an exaggeration understated.

No need to write a great epic: two trout head-to-tail in a frying pan
    make a tragic poem.
A poem is a phosphorescent instant illuminating time, a moment of
    Absolute Spirit.
If the universe or the world had a soul, the aim of poetry would be
    to reveal it.
Poetry is more than painting sunlight on the wall of a house.
It is Van Gogh's ear echoing with all the blood of the world.
It is a lightning rod transmitting epiphanies.
It is a dragonfly catching fire.
It is the sea light of Greece, the diamond light of Greece.
It is a lamp of the imagination lighting up every darkness.
It is a bright vision made dark, a darkling vision made bright.
It's the trees in spring in a back garden on Morton Street.
It is what the late November's saying about the disturbance of the
    spring.
Poems are shadows on the wall of Plato's cave glimpsed but
    fleetingly.
Poetry is eternal graffiti in the heart of everyone.
A poem is a mirror walking down a strange street full of visual
    delight.
Poetry is the shook foil of the imagination; it should shine out and
    half blind you.
It is the sun streaming down in the meshes of morning.
It is white nights and mouths of desire.
It is a tree with live leaves made from log piles of words.
A poem should arise to ecstasy somewhere between speech and song.
Poetry is the still sound between the strings of a lute.
It is the birth of ideas before they are distilled into thought.
It is made by dissolving halos in oceans of sound.
It is the street talk of angels and devils.
It is a sofa full of blind singers who have put aside their canes.
Poems are lifesavers when your boat capsizes.
Poetry is the anarchy of the senses making sense.
It is all things born with wings that sing.
It is a voice of dissent against the waste of words and the mad
    plethora of print.
It is what exists between the lines.

It is made with the syllables of dreams in unwritten dictionaries.

It is far far cries upon a beach at nightfall.

It is a lighthouse moving its megaphone over the sea.

It is a picture of Ma in her Woolworth bra looking out a window into her secret garden.

It is an Arab carrying colored rugs and birdcages through the streets of Baghdad.

A poem can be made of common household ingredients: it fits on a single page yet it can fill a world, and fits in the pocket of a heart.

The poet is a street singer who rescues the alley cats of love in south Yonkers.

Poetry breaks the brass wall between races.

Poems are the lost pages of the books of day & night.

Poetry is the distillation of articulate animals calling to each other across a great gulf.

It is a pulsing fragment of the inner life, an untethered music.

It is the dialogue of naked statues.

It is the sound of gaiety while weeping.

It is the sound of summer in the rain and of people laughing behind closed shutters down an alley at night.

It is Helen's straw hair in sunlight without a permanent.

It is a sword on fire where someone has thrown it to become a pacifist.

It is a bare light bulb in a homeless hotel in Fat City at three in the morning.

It must be more than want ads for broken hearts.

It is worth nothing and therefore invaluable.

It is the incomparable lyric intelligence brought to bear upon fifty-seven varieties of experience.

It is a high house echoing with all the voices that ever said anything crazy or wonderful.

It is a subversive raid upon the forgotten language of the collective unconscious.

It is a real canary in a coal mine, and we know why the caged bird sings.

It is a sounding sea without shores.

It is a rope to tie around you.

It is the shadow cast by our streetlight imaginations.

It is the voice of the Fourth Person Singular.

It is the face behind the face of the race.

It is the voice within the voice of the turtle.

It is the voice of everybody's inscrutable future.

It is made of night-thought; if it can tear itself away from illusion, it
will not be disowned before the dawn.

It is made by evaporating the liquid laughter of youth.

It is a book of light at night dispersing clouds of unknowing.

It hears the whisper of hunted elephants.

It knows how many angels & demons dance on the head of a
phallus.

It is Ulysses' horses mournng his death.

It is a saxophone singing the birth of the blues.

It is a humming, a keening, a laughing, a sighing at dawn, a wild
soft laughter.

It is the final gestalt of the imagination.

It should be emotion recollected in emotion.

Words are living fossils; the poet must piece the skeleton together
and make it sing.

Poetry is perpetual revolt against silence exile and cunning.

It is a guillotine for accepted ideas.

It is a lawless, insurgent enterprise.

The poet a subversive barbarian at the city gates, challenging the
status quo.

It is creative destruction, the poet a master ontologist, forever ques-
tioning reality and reinventing it.

He must be the gadfly of the state mating with a firefly.

He is a pickpocket of reality.

Poetry is a paper boat on the flood of spiritual desolation.

It is the existential dance of the self and the other.

It is the rediscovery of the self against the tribe.

Poems are questions posing further questions.

The poet mixes drinks out of wild liquors and is perpetually sur-
prised that no one staggers.

He is a dark barker before the tents of existence.

He should see the rose through world-colored glasses.

He may be a singing animal turned pimp for an anarchist king.

Poetry is religion, religion poetry.

A poem is a dinghy setting out to sea from the listing ship of society.

A poem is a shadow of a plane fleeing over the ground like a cross escaping a church.

The poem is a telescope waiting for the poet to focus it.

The poet is his own priest and confessor.

Poetry is at once sacred and pagan play at its most utopian.

It is the ludic play of homo ludens.

It is the humming of moths as they circle the flame.

The poet must have wide-angle vision, each look a world glance, and the concrete is most poetic.

He sees eternity in animals' eyes and in the eyes of humans before they look away.

Poetry is not all heroin horses and Rimbaud; it is also the powerless prayers of airline passengers fastening their seatbelts for the final descent.

It is the real subject of great prose.

It speaks the unspeakable, utters the inutterable sigh of the heart.

Each poem a momentary madness, and the unreal is realist.

Poetry a strange form of insanity, tempered by erotic bliss.

A poem should still be an insurgent knock on the door of the unknown

Like a bowl of roses, a poem should not have to be explained.

The lyric poem must rise beyond sounds found in alphabet soup.

Chance is not art, art is not Chance, except by chance.

A poet should be the antennae of his race with more than rabbit ears.

The images in a poem should be *jamais vu*, not *déjà vu*.

Poetry a radical presence, constantly goading us.

The boy scout virtues are still Truth, Beauty, Goodness, Wholeness, Harmony, Radiance.

A sunflower maddened with light sheds the seeds of poems. Some sprout.

Let poetry discover the invisible template of reality, and make it new.

In poetry trees and grasses, beasts and humans try to talk to each other.

Poetry is walking on water, always about to sink.

It gives voice to all who see and sing and laugh and cry.

It is a window through which everything can be seen as never
    before.
Each poem a passionfruit, a pith of pure being.
The poet a trance-dancer in the Last Waltz.
Eyes & lips are the doors of love, sight & sound the portals of poetry.
Poetry a plant growing at night to give a voice to desire.
It is *amore, pan' e vino.*
It's a mediation between everyday reality and us.
It's a meditation that assuages the loneliness of the long-distance
    swimmer.
It serves many masters, not all beatific.
Speech is to poetry as sound is to music, with open tuning.
Poetry is making something out of nothing.
Its function is to debunk with radiant light.
Poetry like love dies hard among the ruins.
Poetry like love a natural painkiller.
It speaks our fears and loves out loud.
It sometimes sees its own shadow at midnight and despairs.
The poet a membrane to filter light and disappear in it.
Poetry a handprint of the invisible, a footprint of visible reality,
    following it like a shadow.
Love delights in love, joy delights in joy, poetry delights in poetry.
For great poetry to be born, there must be *hunger and passion.*
To the lover, it is a pearl; to the hater, it is a thorn.
The mind thinks it knows its way around the heart.
Thinking poetry need not be sans ecstasy.
Poetry is thinking with your skin.
And any child who can catch a firefly owns poetry.
Life itself the greatest tragicomic poem.
And the poet must decide if bird cries are really cries of ecstasy or
    cries of despair.
Poetry a bare ruined choir where last the sweet birds sang.
Poetry the last refuge of humanity in dark times.
And the poet
as the bearer of Eros
as the bearer of love
and pleasure and joy
and total freedom

must by definition
be the natural born
non-violent
enemy of the State,
which would eat
your liberties!"

And thus with the fading of the dusk of dream
did hoary Homer fade away
into American cyberspace
(for he too had migrated
with democracy and slavery)
followed close by Dante and his tour guide Virgil
and others nameless and beardless
spinning wannabe epics
in the broken narrative of human speech
Subtexts of creation
made of babble
The great dialogue
that Plato began
even as Socrates cried, "I drank *what?*"

And in Xanadu did Kubla Khan
hang up a Golden Nail
that held the stars in place
His palaces aligned with it
and the greatest empire in all the world
hung on it
But the sun of time burned off its head
melting down the fine soft gold
Moloch's finest—
And the empire fell into darkness

IV

"*And then went down to the ship,*
                 Set keel to breakers, forth on the godly sea . . ."

What ships what shores what grey islands!
What songs the sirens sang
What name Achilles bore
What harboring Orestes found

     "*So suddenly out of its stale and drowsy lair, the lair of slaves,*
Like lightning Europe lep't forth . . . . . half startled at itself
            Its feet upon the ashes and the rags . . . . . Its hands tight
                 to the throat of kings . . ."

So that—
      we set up mast and sail
                on that swart ship once more
        and so set forth once more
              forth upon the gobbly sea
        loaded with liberated vestal virgins
            and discus throwers reading *Walden*—

And when he was being born in a dream
          he approached the flying earth
              and spied a huge banner stretched 'round it
              like a cloud
              And the sign proclaimed
        ABANDON ALL DESPAIR YE WHO ENTER HERE

Passagio al Occidente
a new kind of passover
And the Genovese sea flooding westward
The high prow parting the spray
una migrazione degli uccelli
following the fantail
crying out *a contrappunto*

With a crew of desperados
and Johan Padan, shanghaied *paisano*—
Full fathom five he falls
(those are pearls that were his balls)

Only connect! cried Columbus
Staring through his telescope
And he scoped it out all right
the "new world" as he saw it
And he saw it plain
made of gold bullion and bloody Marys
And the natives "like children"
brought him treasures they had hoarded
for the next Coming
of Blondie
(described in their *fumetti*
their magic comic strips)
And Johan Padan
topside sailor
Genovese *gióvane*
illiterate *marinaro*
crossed himself and
dropped his pantaloons
when he gazed upon pure flesh of Indy
for the first time
his old time religion
never having prepared him for
naked animal anima
with no sense of sin
quando il verbo si fa carne
As nude virgins and shamans
fell before the blunderbuss
cavalli crashing up the beaches
of Carib paradisos
the gold gleaming heavy
in the blood-red sands

And the great navigator
hugging the absolute shoreline

the great navigator with his lead line
sounding the depths
mapped the continental shelf
ran in at high tide
breaching the shallows
spyglass trained inland
Another body for the human mind
Animus e anima
to be charted probed and bloodlet for gold

> *"Old men carrying their fathers and philosophers*
> *weeping in the dust, America perhaps, Don Quixote"*

And Cortés came
the fair-haired god as prophesied
and was welcomed as such by the *Aztecas*
and so laid waste to them
(although there were later uprisings
at once brave and pathetic—
Tierra y Libertad!
cried an army of Indians
marching out of jungles—
followed still much later by
Viva Zapata!
against the invading powers of Nafta
and the New World Order)

Whereas and wherefor
North of the Border too
Our God the greatest White Father
told the white men under his command
to take all the Indians' land
because that was their manifest destiny
And they did then set forth
with the great obscene hunger of
the territorial imperative—
set forth upon the virgin continent
unmapped uncharted and unsung

And the Mayflower had landed
not in an empty wilderness—
in a land already occupied
with a culture of signs and signals
omens and prophecies—
its pulse later taken by missionary sawbones
bent on converting the heathen
to parlor games, crochet, and high tea

(Boston's Tea Party
the first "people's protest"
against big bad corporations)

While other Whiteys landed up the Hudson
as in a painting of the Hudson River School
wading ashore (also already occupied)
in Dutch boots
to sink in among croaking frogs

History repeats itself with a stutter
Potemkin sailors revolt
Kerensky shoots his bolt
Kropotkin cries
And an anarchist colony is founded at Woodstock

Americus
carrying the contents of civilization
in his hat
Chaplin's beat-up bowler
And the world his melon
balanced on his head

So that—he a man of no fortune
with naught to lose
and much to gain—
A wop and a yid in one
A kind of Don Quixote

tilting at sawmills and ginmills
A Euro man indeed
(Blackie and Whitey and all shades in between)
on the virginous land
as American as Booker T. Washington
or brother Du Bois (who had no use for him)
or Emma Goldman or Mother Jones
or Walt Whitman or Mark Twain
"the Lincoln of our lit"
Each a palimpsest of everybody's past
A man like a country
Restless . . . driven . . .
And the forest birds shaken with music

In the gloaming
by a waterfall
a woman shakes out her gold hair
Across the pond
his heart turns over
Lovely stranger, life is fleeting—
If we could know each other!
Darkness falls

V

To write a Republic, then—
to write of the first and last people
the tales of the tribe writ down
                          and washed away
            figures in sand
                          blown away
                or erased with a sweep of the hand

Ourselves (the interlopers)
in Blueberry America
inhabiting our own imagination
                          Eakins' single scullers still rowing
                          on the upper Hudson
                          of our dreaming lives
            And the Catskills still
                raising their stone battlements

Achaean into American
The peasant leads his horse
through blackberry kingdoms
and comes out at a crossroads
in North America
(the name *America* itself
usurped from *Las Americas*
by Anglos)

And journalism a rough draft of history
written by billions of scriveners
and revised later to suit
by victors and owners of everything
For who controls the present
controls the past

CAPT. DREYFUS FRENCH ARMY TRAITOR
DEGRADED AND DEPORTED
Sent to Devils Island for Life
"J'Accuse!" Screams Émile Zola

FLEETS MAY MEET IN LUZON BATTLE TODAY

OIL KING'S HAPPIEST DAY
BLOODY SUNDAY IN MOSCOW
CZAR GRANTS CONSTITUTION
Peasants Suspicious

WAR & PEACE ALL AT ONCE!
"War the Death of the Soul"

Author of "Souls of Black Folk"
W.E.B. DU BOIS JAILED AGAIN

Whereas—the people wrote their own history
With the help of Howard Zinn, to wit:
Columbus and the Indians
Persons of Mean and Vile Condition
Tyranny and a Kind of Revolution
and the Intimately Oppressed
and Slavery without Submission
and Emancipation without Freedom
and The Other Civil War
and Robber Barons and Rebels
and The Empire and the People
and The Socialist Challenge
and War as the Health of the State
and Self-help in Hard Times
and a People's War
and an Impossible Victory
and the Bipartisan Concencus
and the Unreported Resistance
and the Revolt of the Guards
and the—

(And Tocqueville was so wrong
but more of that later)

    While they were changing guards at Buckingham Palace and
Christopher Robin went down with Alice, and Queen Victoria an old
lady in a pointed lace cap sent chocolate to the soldiers at Christmas.
The failed plot against her said to have been perpetrated by a cell of
Irish anarchist shipyard workers wearing the red badge of anarchy
on their coats and supplied with beer . . .

COURT SETS ZOLA FREE

NATION GREETS CENTURY'S DAWN
Fireworks Over the Capitol
Ferris Wheel Burns!
Seen as Symbolic

GAIETY GIRLS ARRESTED IN NEW JERSEY

"IT TAKES NERVE TO LOVE IN THIS WORLD"
LAST WORDS OF GEORGE SMITH
HANGED WITH HIS BROTHER BY MOB

MARQUIS OF QUEENSBERRY DEAD

POET WALT WHITMAN DIES
He heard America singing

Spring dusk dark shore
Long Island New York April
Sky over Patchogue dense and grey
as Whitman's beard
Flights of grey geese
nested in it
over hulk of his fair body—
'Fishshape Paumanok—'
Hulk of him hove-to

off old Mannahatta
Poets still swim off of it
their far cries failing
like lost sailors in a burning
Turner shipwreck—
Red sun flames through
On the very shores of light!

TELL HOW THEY FLEW!
Wright Brothers Give Account
Of Airship Test in North Carolina
SOARED AGAINST A GALE

The men at the launch rail realized Wilbur was not going to come back to the ground right away. The machine was leaving them far behind—200, 400, 600 feet, the noise of the engine fading, the wings on an even keel. He was flying!

So that—Over a hundred years ago, when all the machines began to hum, the Wright brothers thought they had invented something that could make peace on earth (if the wrong brothers didn't get hold of it) when their wonderful flying machine took off at Kitty Hawk—

So that—was it already too late to ask
too naively
that an insatiable gaiety
rule the earth
too much to hope
too blindly
that someday there might be
A dearth of death—
"The past a mess of blood and sorrow"
Is not some gross national happiness
still possible?
the human spirit reanimated?
Could a hero or antihero still emerge

from the calamity of humanity?
Where is the splendid antique structure
the centered figure
the great new *spielmann*
speaking with tragicomic voice
shaking the wings
of his 'exultant and terrible youth'
(as James Joyce cried out
on the last page of his *Portrait*
leaving home and mother and Dublin 1904
"to forge in the smithy" of his soul
"the uncreated conscience" of his race)

And was there not one moment in time
when our liberated adventurer
might have felt himself to be
a new unique form of life on earth
Was there not one moment when he felt
a quivering a wavering vibe
between himself and all breathing beings
and a deep ineffable delight
engulfing him
as if he were not a man separate and apart
from the rest of creation
but a part of pure nature
without the hubris to destroy it—

OUT FOR BULLY GOOD TIME
New Year's Gaiety in Gotham

WORLD'S GREATEST SEA BATTLE NEAR

DISGRACED!
Oscar Wilde Jailed as Pervert
Sent to Reading Gaol

And all of this taking place
on one small ball of earth
like some kind of work-in-progress
by some puttyball sculptor
or nightmaze novelist
A crazy scene to hitchhike into
landing on a Rand McNally globe
with compass roses looking like real islands
and trees towers telephones
bridges bedsprings rivers
fountains and crosses
sprouting out of it
as it whirls around
disgorging strings of colored lights
rockets popbottles candy and cigarettes
like an enormous IBM automat hung in space
and run by solar energy
And all of it held together with light and bones
and roots and mud and bubble gum and tar
and jass and jizm and spit and skin and reinforced concrete
and skeins of yarn and clotheslines
and hope and clay
And the whole scene turning and turning
through the soundless wingless air
like some huge store-window carrousel
with a Special Clearance Sale of Famous Masterpieces
Including one replica of Rodin's Thinker with hand on chin
pondering the insoluble problem
next to one bronze head of Albert Einstein
next to a megaphone mask of a Muse of Tragedy
next to a fragment of a medieval crucifix
with the painted wood head of Christ
next to a biblical painting of Adam
sitting under a denuded fig tree
with one rib missing and a bitten apple in his hand
for the first time pondering the insoluble problem
next to a painted bust of Queen Nefertiti
next to one disarmed Venus de Milo

next to Whistler's Mother rocking and rocking
next to one white unicorn in captivity
next to a wooden model of the Trojan Horse
with clay men inside with hands on chins
pondering the insoluble problem
next to a watercolor Jonah inside his whale
next to a rubber working model of the Great White
with Ahab on his back
with one leg missing and hand on chin
next to a gift edition of Shakespeare
open to an illustration of Hamlet
with chinless Yorick in his hand
pondering the insoluble problem
next to a cardboard Lincoln Memorial
with Lincoln inside
pondering the insoluble problem
next to a painting of Washington Crossing the Delaware
standing in the boat against Navy regulations
next to a hollow Buddha with holes in head
through which incense smokes
above and beyond the insoluble problem
that only 'love' might somehow solve

VI

All Quiet on the Western Front
(all quiet because all dead)
and *Slaughterhouse Five*
alive inside a freezer
in the fire-bombing of Dresden

Verdun or Dresden
Dun the color of dun
Dres the color of dread

      DARK DAWN OF INHUMAN WAR
          A New Kind of Killing
          Men vs. Machines

          "Shock and Awe"

      BOTH SIDES REEL

General says "Gettysburg Nothing Like This"

VERDUN! VERDUN! under relentless fire without any protection
except   for the narrow trench   Arrived with 175 men and
returned with 34 of whom several had half turned insane com-
panies of skeletons passed sometimes commanded by a wounded
officer leaning on a stick. *In war we become speechless faces
Mein Liebchen*   Horrors of their martyrdom. They must be
crazy to do what they are doing now

Over there!
        Over there!

The Yanks are coming
        Over there!

What a bloodbath what horrid images, *The comradeship of war is a strange form of love.* Hell cannot be this dreadful. An awful word, Verdun. People still young and filled with hope. *In wartime a soldier's life is especially pleasant. Only in battle does a man attain his full stature* They lay down their lives here   *mein liebe Marlene* their mortal remains decomposing *A weird form of love this comradeship We suddenly no longer feel alone*

To Carthage then I came . . . Burning burning burning

Woe betide anyone who falls into the hands of the enemy alive; all sense of humanity disappeared. Already I feel within me the lust to sink my teeth in the enemy's throat   In the ecstatic bliss of war Comrades lose their identity in this euphoria   Human beings? Their monument an ossiary an acre full of bones

         It's a long way to Tipperary It's a long way to go
Near Le Mort-Homme a corpse afloat in it

In the dying days of that far summer
              when we climbed the hill
                      and lay in the sun
                             and made love in the tall grasses

In war we no longer have to face death alone   We have our buddies Comradeship! The Three Musketeers! We'll save each other, die together, birds of a feather   without feathers

Mein liebe Mutter
                Sing me a song sing me a song
        Mein lieber Hans
                      The body dreams but does not sleep
We will become as air
              as darkness

In a closed house not opened since the turn of the century   the doors are not where they were and homeland is no longer home

Mein Liebchen
    Summers we went to the mountains
                      the air
                         was free

Look look the horse has lost its head The house is gone   carrying us
    with it They keep coming and coming the brown troops the gray
    troops the black uniforms in steel helmets pointed helmets my god
    we're being run over the tanks the blitzers the mustard . . . shit
    I'll lie down somewhere hide somewhere I'll die We're not brave
    we're

      Summers we spent in the mountains
                      In the winters we went south
                  Flowers on the river in winter
                      In the mountains you feel free
                        Mein Liebchen

There is even hardly enough strength left to pray   These are not
humans coming and coming   How much longer   If only If only
night would come and cover us good
  Confusion and clash of consciences!   *War is always betrayal*

    The trenches a network of pits where the nightly shits pile up
Consequences of a flame-thrower attack *Betrayal of the young by
the old*   Some grenadiers with ghastly wounds: hair and *eyebrows
burned off, not human anymore, black creatures with bewildered eyes
LUMPEN PROLETARIUM SCUM! The weight of the world is hate*
At my feet two unlucky creatures rolled on the floor their guts out
    Living torches. They set each other on fire, fired on each other
We have become the company we keep   so mutilated that we could
    not decide on their identities. *We are our own enemy Brother
    against brother*   In a fit of insanity the other hummed a tune
    from his childhood
                Behind the wagon we flung him in
talked to his wife and his mother and spoke of his village. Seven days
    of fear
          made these healthy men into bewildered beasts.

War is a poison we must ingest, as cancer patients must ingest
    cancer to be cured
       Commanded by a blinded Captain, the men stumbled forward
  or backward.   *Betrayal of the people by the people by their*
leaders The blind captain asked blindly   which company
                                 we were in

    and then started to
             cry all of a sudden
                  Marie! Marie!

"Sophocles long ago
Heard it on the Aegean
. . . the turbid ebb and flow
Of human misery . . . "

       Ach, mein Liebchen, let us be true to one another

Loveliest of trees
The cherry now
Is hung with dung along the bough
And stands along the woodland ride
Wearing black for Eastertide

       The earth moves and shakes like jelly   Screams
    of hurt
              horses,
                    J'ai rêvé tellement fort de toi . . .

     "Desiring still my head
           Between your breasts"

    The wild pounding of our hearts under fire
             hour after hour night after after
       Reich mir die Hand, mein Leben, Komm auf mein
  Schloss mit mir . . .
Soldiers fell over like tin soldiers *Plague of Nationalism* They
quenched their thirst with water from shell holes *Mankind is kept*
alive by bestial acts. The exhilaration of mass killing Eros and
Thanatos compete for prizes

I will show you fear in a handful of shit
Chers amis, mes chers compatriots   numbed by seeing the bodies
     without heads without legs shot through
blown away foreheads Memory gone   *Dearest Suzie*   Search for
     cover in a shell hole full of slime
                    Hollow ghosts in hellfields they fall in each others' arms
Their uniforms no longer different Both sides the color of manure
We killed *The Grand Illusion* the Old Lie: Dulce et decorum est Pro
     Patria Mori!

Over there, over there, the Yanks are coming, over there . . .

                    Who   says
                         Every   war   is   a
                              failure   of   civilization

'O waste of loss,
in the hot mazes, lost,
among bright stars
on this most weary unbright cinder . . . '

God, come back, innocence of the world,
A song, a line, a free phrase
in autumn capitals
their avenues of leaves ablaze

          I ain't gonna study
                    ain't gone study
                              war no more
          I gonna lay down
                    my sword and shield
     I ain't gonna study
                    War no more
     I ain't gonna study
                    war no more

"And what is that *anima*, what is it exactly that drives men forward
(or backward), if it is not just pure desire, raw wanting, raw hunger

35

for everything and anything, sexual and spiritual, driving man to create, to create other beings in the image of loved ones, or other earthworks and skyscrapers and far-flung bridges spanning the unknown, and great roads, endless highways, over the horizon? Yes, we all love creating roads into the wilderness, but then why do we also love destruction so much? War and destruction and chaos! *Dopo noi il caos!* When we're almost there, when we've almost finished building the Crystal Palace, the shining edifice we are to live in, in perfect harmony in a perfect society—Why, then—let's just have a little war and blow it all up, so that we can begin all over again, from the beginning! Could it be that man has such a love because he is secretly afraid of achieving that goal beyond which is nothing—?"

" World War1 the human race stinks
 World War 2 the human race shrinks
 World War 3 the human race extincts"

Prisoners of history
bound hand and foot!
we weep to hear again
those sirens sing again
over the wrong rivers
Deutschland über alles
Unter den Linden

And Adolph played footsie with Ludwig
                    in Austrian grammar school
      Austriche paperhanger
            In Jude gymnasium
                  with classmate Wittgenstein
                     son of industry giant
                        steel mills and railroads
                                    larger than Krupp
                  darlink boy
                           Ach, who could touch him?

And the Germans became German Expressionists as the Blue Rider rode over The Bridge into the Bauhaus on more than one blue horse And Franz Marc made his blue mark And Kirchner cantered through the dark circus on a different dark horse And Emil Nolde danced boldly around a golden calf And Max Pechstein fished in river landscapes and fooled around with his models (They all did that) And Rottluff painted his rusty lust And Otto Mueller ate cruellers as his painting grew crueler And Erich Heckel heckled himself with madmen and thereby foresaw their mad ends And Norwegian Munch let out a silent scream And Jawlensky made Matisse look mad and Russian And Kandinsky grew insanely incandescent And Kokoschka drew his own *sturm und drang* And Käthe Kollwitz chalked the face of Death and the Mother And Schwitters twittered through trash cities And Klee became a clay mobile swaying to the strains of the Blue Angel And Otto Dix drew a dying warrior on his steely palette And Grosz glimpsed the grossest in the gathering storm And Max Beckmann saw the sinking of the Titanic And Meidner painted the Apocalypse And Feininger traced a Tragic Being and fingered skyscrapers that fell across the Atlantic (and the Bauhaus in its final antic fell on Chicago) While meanwhile back in Berlin Hitler was painting himself into a corner And his ovens were heating as a Tin Drum began beating

VII

"In 1793, whether the mood of the day was good or bad, idealist or fanatic, the masses poured out of the Faubourg Saint-Antoine both barbaric and heroic. Barbaric! What did they want, these bristling men, dressed in rags, howling, ferocious, bludgeons raised, brandishing pikes, in those pregnant days of revolutionary chaos, pouring down the old Paris boulevards, what did they want? They wanted the end of oppression, tyrannies, the two-edged sword, they wanted work for men, education for children, calm security for women, liberty, equality, fraternity, bread for all, freedom of thought for all, the Edenizing of the world, they wanted Progress, that hallowed, good, and gentle thing, progress, pushed to the limit, beyond themselves— they clamored for it, terrible, half-nude, bludgeons in their fists, red at the lips. Savages, yes; but savages of civilization . . . forcing the human race toward Paradise . . . . "

Could we wish humanity different?
Could we wish the people made of wood and stone?
Or that there be no justice in destiny or time?

And Marcel Proust took to his cork-lined chambers and started remembering his Things Past to recapture lost time, and for a long time he went to bed early, "Longtemps, je me suis couché à la bonne heure"— and obsessively created his *haute monde et demimonde*, a whole belle universe where we did wander enchanted within a budding grove along Swann's Way to a Guermantes soirée

La vida es sueño

Whereas by the Twenties the first American invasion of Paris was already on, along the avenues the tour buses filled with them, and guides pointing out monuments, and the Yanks going "Wow!" And Gert Rude Stein busy Making Americans . . . She, who wrote as a child speaks, had turned her back on the Newer World and taken off backwards, to Gay Paree and then provincial France where no one could comprehend a word of her American (French she spoke like a pelican) and *The Making of Americans* her master pun (on the run from Alice who held the chalice) she seldom uttered the word American in a thousand pages except in thinking about thinking of anything or anybody who goes anywhere and is an American and is strictly American to carry within them huge spaces in time filled with moving for they are always moving and moving isn't it true too true Alice says so and thus she said she herself could *describe every type of human being* in making Americans always moving and moving and removing for it must be remembered whether it's Chinamen or Americans they are the same kinds of men and women amen and women moving women moving men moving women restless searching she said I am always wondering wondering how long we can go on searching is there an end of searching no end of it Alice said in bed is not life a hiding why are we hiding hiding always here, we are here today, goners tomorrow, here with the Boches are we hiding, we are just living, Roasted Suzie is my ice cream We know nothing Jews are not enemies Tell them my Cherman is better than my French fries oh Alice tell them tell them Gertrude went down with Alice when they were changing guards at Élysées Palace and they had their Faÿ ways oh are not guards always changing changing and Faÿ has ways . . .

> Oh I'm a Yankee Doodle dandy
> A Yankee do or die
> A real live nephew of my Uncle Sam
> Born on the Fourth of July!

Whereas Jimmy Joyce felt "the spell of arms and voices: the white arms of roads . . . " yet never set pen in America North or South, much to his impoverishment (and ours), having quite enough nourishment at the ear or teat of Anna Livia or Molly, hardly needing our folly to explicate his uncreated consciousness

While Virginia the Woolf posited that "in or about 1910 human character changed" And Hepburn "born to play Jo" in *Little Women* went on for half a century playing herself, embodying the strengths and frailties of a new breed of woman

Whereas Henry Miller from Brooklyn in his Air-Conditioned
Nightmare many years later exclaimed "another breed of men has
taken over. "

Wrapped in the coils of your own long night
(believe it or not, cher poète
there is a world outside yourself)

And I am not familiar
with the exact constitution of the Tarot pack of cards,
quoth the Tsetse fly, filing his nails,
But I do know a thing or three
about Hanged Men in Bloomsbury drawing rooms

> *The last time I saw Paris*
>> *Her heart was warm and gay*

Absinthe lover full of absence
The tremor of your voice
among the violins
your eyes elsewhere
your hyacinth hair your naiad airs
in old Europa
"Et sous le Pont Mirabeau coule la Seine
And our loves too
Must I remember them again"

Dietrich in *Blue Angel*
Garbo in *Anna Karenina*
Proust and his madeleine
Apollinaire's migraine
Afternoons on the Grande Jatte
The arrogance of André Breton
And the parody of *Le Paradis Artificiel*
And Little Addie the housepainter
with the toothbrush moustache
Is Paris burning?
And it's *Au revoir, les enfants*

Jonny, Dietrich sings in German,
Jonny when your birthday comes
I'll be your guest all night
Jonny I love you so much
If you only had a birthday every day
How about coming some afternoon at four?

While the Valkyries were singing
Unter den Linden

Lilli Marlene Lilli Marlene
            Underneath the lamplight
                        By the village green

And the weight of the world could still be love

Marie, Marie, hold on tight—

But a Blue Rider appears
and the light changes

A shower of crystal
a rain of crystal
in Kristallnacht
followed by a loud dead silence
Some heard the silence of the sea
Some drank Vichy
Some were shot running
Some were hung against a wall
Some died singing

Quand on est dans la merde jusqu'au cou, il ne reste plus qu' à
    chanter

LES PATROUILLES AMERICAINES ONT PENETRE
EN ALLEMAGNE

LES PREMIERES DEFENSES DE LA LIGNE SIEGFRIED
ONT ETE PERCEES

La Visite du General de Gaulle et de M. Churchill
A la 1re Armée française

L'INDUSTRIE ALLEMANDE ECRASEE
PAR LES BOMBES ALLIEES

Et c'est toujours Saint-Germain
J'entends encore la voix palpitante
de l'accordion dans le metro
l'hiver quarante-quatre
Où je sens encore
les Gauloises Jaunes
et la voix américaine
le Latin de nos jours
Mais je suis toujours occupé
Occupé des rêves-pensées
Qui me disent toujours
que la vie toujours
et noble et tragique . . .

Rappelle-toi Barbara

Rappelle-toi Bar-ba-ra . . .

Quelle connerie la guerre . . .

VIII

A hopefulness without frontiers
A feeling of joy and openness
upon alighting in America
(a bird flown over)

Lady Liberty with flaming torch
stands upon her little island

And they came beaten
escaping slaveries
starved of body and soul
faces drawn in shawls
on deck sighting Liberty
(as seen by Edward Steichen)

On Ellis Island he saw her
   Hair of seaweed
         against the sun silhouetted
  Not an idol in an idyll
        but a black & white photo
           of an Irish Anna Livia
               descending a gangplank
      hair falling down
        around a face full of hunger
           in great potato famines
    And whose mother did she become
        in the wide womb of America?

So into Brooklyn Queens the Bronx and Harlem
And it's Goodbye, Columbus, and Run Rabbit Run
Or striking westward at once
with five dollars a cardboard suitcase
and an address of someone gone before
lost relatives refound or never found
in Appalachia—

or striking south to the Carolinas or Georgia
"lives haunted by a Georgia slattern
because a London cutpurse went unhung"

A crowd flows over Brooklyn Bridge
The quays black with refugees
They took to the streets
They worked at anything
They swarmed everywhere
They scratched to get a foothold anywhere
to feed their mouths

Pleaza mistah—No squeeza da banane—Squeeza da cocanut

Driving a cardboard automobile
without a license
at the turn of the century
his father ran into his mother
on a fun ride at Coney Island
Having spied each other eating
in a French boardinghouse nearby
and having decided right there and then
that she was for him entirely
he followed her
into the playland of that evening
where the headlong meeting
of their ephemeral flesh on wheels
hurtled them forever together . . .

furbo Lombardo
(via Marseille or Bordeaux)
Auctioneer and small-time *mafioso*
in Little Italy
then conceived a son in sun
on a Sunday picnic by the Hudson
as in a painting of the Hudson River School

And many years later the son
goes back and finds the house where he was born—
It must have been all country back then
And the kids playing stickball
Their far cries echoing
In this green meadow
with its worn baseball diamond
with rocks for bases
and its ancient rusted screen
behind the batter's box
He could still hear the bat hit the ball
(perhaps hit by Pop)
his brother running for first base
and ending up in Baltimore
forty years later

Echoed shouts and laughter fill the air

And then the famous Spirit of St. Louis *took off eastward and flew
across the Big Pond with Lindy at the controls in his leather helmet
and goggles hoping to sight the doves of peace but he did not Even
though he circled Versailles—*

Pause and begin again—
Flappers flap in the Nineteen Twenties
The *Hindenburg* burns the Market crashes
and it's *"Yes, we have no bananas"*
and "Time Marches On"
FDR's Fireside Chat on every Motorola
On the radio it's Orson Welles
over the sound of panic & pandemonium
the invasion from Mars!

He still a barefoot boy on a canoe trip on the great river—Ah how the
Hudson burned in Indian autumn—
                    Saugerties
                            Coxsackie
                                    fell away through
                                            all those trees

Bicyclists among the trees by the lake Piano music slow in the distance The summer air is heavy with desiring The future lover winds through the woods trailing her purple scarf toward her future lover Or a girl in a long white dress and a picture hat strolls across a lawn to Gatsby It's all an unfinished film for which there is no finis (so we would like to think) seen through a telephoto lens in which the future couple will have future children in real time who will run through the woods each to his or her own future And they reproduce themselves and they are multiplied a trillion trillion trillion times And the film-loop runs on and on and on and on with many a retake And as through the wrong end of a telescope we see the myriad antic figures forever disappearing over the far horizon As if the quivering meat-wheel tape (we would like to think) could never break

How the light lay on the leaves
How the light glinted through them
In the dawn of the world that year
How the leaves themselves
were light
How all creatures there
were light
were made of light
the warp of light
upon them
And they pulsed with it
with light of earth
as if they would always be
full of light
made of light
shimmering
among the sere and yellow leaves

In the autumn of that year

He still playing stickball by Bronx River Parkway . . . and where is that little fish he caught and left on the line still swimming in the still stream under that little bridge when he was nine, meaning to return? Swept away! And he with it, in flood of time

PIMLICO MADNESS!
Run-up to the Greatest Horse Race in History

*America hangs in midair, the names War Admiral and Seabiscuit
on everyone's lips. The raucous division between the horses'
supporters becoming a fanatical contest of East versus West, the
Wild West Seabiscuit against the Virginia patrician War Admiral,
a Civil War raging between them . . . .*

Meanwhile back in New York
Queens' huge cemetery
in setting sun
by Long Island's old expressway
(once a dirt path for wheelless Indians)
myriad small tombstones tilted up
gesturing statues on parapets
stone arms or wings upraised
lost among illegible inscriptions
The setting yellow sun
painting all of them
on one side only
with an ocher brush
Rows and rows and rows
of small stone slabs
tilted toward the sun forever
On the far horizon
Mannahatta's great stone slabs
(the architecture makes the people)
skyscraper tombs and temples
casting their own long black shadows
over all these long-haired graves
the final restless places of
spics and wops and dagos and polacks
hunkies and sheenies and krauts
Sephardic yids and high yallers
blacks and browns and anglos
fellahs and mullahs Kurds and Sikhs
Moroccan *haschin* and desert sheiks

Irish micks and potato farmers
dustbin pawnbrokers
midtown clothing-district rabbis
Dublin bouncers and bobbies
tinsmiths and blacksmiths and roofers
house painters and house carpenters
cabinetmakers and cigar rollers
garment workers and streetcar motormen
railroad switchmen and signal salesmen
black lawyers and black swabbers and swampers
steamfitters and keypunch operators
ward heelers and labor organizers
railroad dicks and *mafiosi*
shopkeepers and saloon keepers and doormen
icemen and middlemen and con men
Irish housekeepers and housewives and dowagers
French governesses and Swedish cooks
Brooklyn barmaids and Bronxville butlers
opera singers and gandy dancers
pitchers and catchers
in the days of ragtime baseball
poolroom hustlers and fight promoters
Catholic sisters of charity
parish priests and Irish cops
Viennese doctors of delirium
All abandoned now
to eternity
parcels in a dead-letter office
inscrutable addresses on them
beyond further deliverance
in an America wheeling past them
and disappearing
westward
oblivious
into East River's echoing tunnels
down the great American drain . . .

While the sun in America
also rises

And there is a garden
in the memory of America
There is a night bird in its memory

With Ti-Jean Kerouac
On the banks of the Merrimack
In Thirty Seven's flood
haunted by his Doctor Sax
his awesome amanuensis
And the dusk falling

Even as Anton Dvorák's Symphony
strikes up a for a new world
(what he heard of it
with Euro ears)
sounding the great promise
and the huddled masses
still longing for it
A bent Utopian dream
a kind of mirage over the horizon

> *While in his dream he was lover-boy*
> *and her lips as hard as stale bread*
> *until he softened them with his . . .*

> *Love me baby love me love me*
> *All my dreams fulfill . . .*

"Good evening, Mr. & Mrs. North and South America and all the
ships and clippers at sea . . ."

SELF-STYLED LOVER OF MANKIND
HANGS HIMSELF

Tragedy Everlasting:
NATION STILL MOURNS
LINDBERGHS' LOST CHILD

HIGH SOCIETY BROUGHT TO EARTH:
'GREAT GATSBY' SHOT IN SWIMMING POOL

PEARL HARBOR HORROR!
JAPS' "SURPRISE" ATTACK
"A Day That Will Live in Infamy"

NAVY CHAPLAIN'S PRAYER:
Praise the Lord and pass the ammunition!

U-BOAT PASSES AMBROSE LIGHT UNDETECTED

BILLIONS FOR ALLIES
Lend Lease, Lend Lose?

"Nothing to fear but fear itself"
Claims FDR

Dearest One,

I seem to have loved you in infinite forms, in life after life, age after age forever. My entranced heart has made and remade this necklace of songs I send to you now, which you can wear in your many forms, in life after life, age after age.

You and I have floated on the stream that springs from the fount of love for one another, old love, but in shapes that are renewed forever and forever, universal joy, universal sorrow, universal life, the memories of everybody's love merging with this one love of ours—

LOOSE LIPS SINK SHIPS

DOS PASSOS PUBLISHES *USA*
The 42nd Parallel
The Big Money
1919

Oh if I had the wings of an angel
                    Over these prison walls I would fly

Italian-American Agony:
Despite World-Wide Demonstrations
SACCO & VANZETTI EXECUTED!

IF iT HAD NOT BEEN FOR THESE THiNG,
I MiGHT HAVE LiVE OUT MY LiFE TALK-
iNG AT STREET CORNERS TO SCORN-
iNG MEN. I MIGHT HAVE DiE, UN-
MARKED, UNKNOWN, A FAILURE. NOW
WE ARE NOT A FAILURE. THIS IS OUR
CAREER AND OUR TRIUMPH. NEVER IN
OUR FULL LiFE COULD WE HOPE TO
DO SUCH WORK FOR TOLERANCE, FOR
JOOSTiCE, FOR MAN'S ONDERSTANDiNG
OF MAN AS NOW WE DO—OUR WORDS—
OUR LiVES—OUR PAiNS—
NOTHING! THE TAKiNG OF OUR LiVES—
LiVES OF A GOOD SHOEMAKER AND A
POOR FiSH PEDDLER—ALL! THAT LAST
MOMENT BELONGS TO US—THAT
AGONY IS OUR TRIUMPH.

The girls in their summer dresses
                    Left me behind
        O blow, blow thou winter wind unkind . . . .

And Gustav Mahler leading to Schoenberg
in Nineteen Thirties Hollywood
Their musicks the sound of the decline & fall
as prophesied long before by Hërr Spengler
And Schoenberg's American sound the Bauhaus sound
strained through a sheet
run through the Nazi wringer
with jazz pianos and cocaine flutes
in an age still struggling to be born
even as America ate its young

Whilst in 1942 Alfred Kazin equated
the rise of modern American lit
with America's coming of age
"Twenty or thirty years ago,
when all the birds began to sing
(almost, as it seemed, in chorus)"

And American poesie
having survived the defeated romanticism
of Prufrock and his pathetic phallusies
now took on the great sound of greater Manhattan
and the boheme Village
with booze at Chumley's
or McSorley's Wonderful Saloon
or ale at the White Horse Tavern
(where Dylan Thomas later drank
the rest of his life away)
while all the while down south
a Tate-worm was eating away
at American letters

While up at Yale the Whiffenpoofs still were singing
To the tables down at Mory's
To the place where Louey dwells
To the good old Temple Bar
We love so well—
Gentlemen songsters out on a spree

Gone from here to eternity
We are poor little lambs
who have lost our way
We are poor little sheep
Who have gone astray
Baa baa baa . . .

While in the mansions of Bronxville they are playing bridge and lis-
tening to Lowell Thomas on the radio: "So long until tomorrow."

Downtown, Parkway Road, Bronxville, by the railroad tracks, he
now in a Sea Scout troop. They are 13-year-old sailors aboard an
imaginary warship chalked on the gym floor. Everyone salutes and
practices knots and splices. An old mate lays on them his lore, his
half-thumb showing what not to do with a line in a cleat, his tattoos
attesting to many a drunk night ashore.

Come on and hear Come on and hear Alexander's Ragtime Band

Come on and hear Come on and hear It's the best band in
the land . . .

On a weekend excursion train a year later, he sees the Connecticut
River flooding, carrying houses chicken coops and carcasses. A cow
stands on the slanting roof of a floating barn. Farmers and farmers'
sons sit on the banks, watching their world float by. The train creaks
on, the dusk is falling. His face pressed against the moving window,
he sees the wide brown river flowing, the heavy-headed trees, the rut-
ted lanes, lone figures at crossings (they wave)—

IX

So that—then suddenly it's ten or twelve years later, and they were so young and didn't know it, and they were sailing a ship into the teeth of it. They were thirty men and three officers on a 110-foot diesel-powered wooden-hulled subchaser, the *USS SC1308*. It was a great sea boat and could go through anything. And did.

It was his first command, after three and a half years on similar vessels—convoy escorts on the North Atlantic—as third officer and then second-in-command. And in his late teens he had worked on scallop boats or other wood hulls out of Gloucester and met the sea in many a nor'easter, ice on the rigging in the worst of it. He was now 25 or '6, and there was salt on his braid. He handled the ship at sea as if he'd been at it all his young life. He was good at it, with the blood of some ancestor like Amerigo Vespucci, navigator on Medici expeditions, discoverer of South America 1499. He was a part of the sea, and the sea was a part of him. The sea was in his blood, and he took to it, a sea creature.

It was before dawn, June 6, 1944, and they were blacked out as part of a convoy escort and antisubmarine screen. Out of Plymouth, England, they were steaming in formation, east northeast in the English Channel, toward the beaches of Normandy, signal flags were streaming from yardarms in the high wind.

Two nights before in Plymouth, the deep country lanes between hedgerows clogged with heavy transport and troops, loaded weapons carriers, thousands and thousands of soldiers in battle gear, all blacked out and silent. And in the whispering fields all around, great encampments, whole armies bivouacked in tents, with small hooded cooking fires.

And it was the night before Agincourt, the young king visiting his men around campfires in the muffled dark.

Now it was 4 or 5 a.m. on the blacked-out bridge of the *USS SC1308*, the first light just cracking the eastern horizon, the whole crew in life jackets and helmets at battle stations. Exec Officer Gene Feinblatt on the bridge with him, Third Officer Doug Crane below in the engine room, the pancake diesels sending up a steady hum. And in the very first light on the western horizon astern, they were just beginning to see a forest of masts rising up, first just the top of masts and then the dark hulls—a huge armada of thousands of great ships and troop transports and escort vessels steaming together from separate ports, converging with first light off the Normandy coast, waves of Allied bombers going high over toward "Utah" and "Omaha" beaches still shrouded in darkness, and then distant explosions on the coast becoming a roar in the dark, as the men stood at their stations, Gene in his life jacket and helmet, red hair showing, binoculars trained on the French coast just coming into range in the dawn, the armada steaming full ahead for the beaches now, dead ahead.

And fair stood the wind for France!

The profound smell of the sea
in your matted hair
Manina
rider to the sea
The sands were hot
where we lay
that halcyon day
forever and forever

Kensington Plaza Garages, Inc.
Main Office—42 Palmer Avenue
Bronxville, N.Y.

January 19, 1944

Dear Admiral:

Just scratch of the pen, my boy, to enclose two very important letters to you. One from Uncle Sam asking you to share your large Income with him and the other a V-Mail letter to Madame, wrote to you under date of November 5th, 1943, which returned here unsealed, as you will note.

Our hearts were repaired and made exceedingly glad by your letter of January 13th, for we had begun to worry about you, fearing you were out sinking subs, sub rosa, as it had been such a long time since we had received anything informative from you to cheer the old home and fireside.

We have everything well in hand (as since you left nothing got out of hand, that I know of) not even Bonnie having escaped for a round of the Village.

It is very mild here almost like spring, probably much warmer than where you are floating at present.

Drop us a post card or line from time to time as we get a little anxious about you when we do not hear from you more frequently.

Cheerio, I'll B.Cing you before long I hope and with lotions of best wishes from us both, I remain your true friend and well wisher,

—General *Bisland (ret)*

Albertine Albertine
          Sephardic and Catholic
                    French Portuguese American
          Years later still spoke French to him
                              Long time ago

                    Albertine Albertine

                                        Long time ago . . . .
God
          he had forgotten how the Hudson burns in Indian autumn
                    The leaves die turning
                              fallen falling
                                        into loam of dark
                    yellow into death
                              disappearing
          fallen fallen falling
                              —those 'pestilence-stricken multitudes'
                    rushed into the streets
                                        blown all blasted
They are hurting them with wood rakes
                    They are raking them in great hills
     They are burning them
                              the leaves curl burning
                    the curled smoke
                              gives up to eternity

Never never the same leaf
                    turn again
                              the same leaves burn
       Lord lord in a red field
                         a white stallion stands
              and pees his oblivion
                         upon those leaves
       Lord lord
                    never returning
                         the long years fallen away back then—

HERE DOWN ON DARK EARTH
Before we all go to Heaven
VISIONS OF AMERICA
All that hitchhikin
       All that railroadin . . . .

And thus did he see first the dark land

A crowd flows over Williamsburg Bridge, Irish and Jewish and East Euros fight for the turf. Coffee steams in the ancient diner by the bridge. It's been there forever already.

Bottom of Manhattan, at the Bowery Mission, the bums are lining up as usual for the evening feed. (Copies of the *Catholic Worker* passed out by Dorothy Day and Ammon Hennessey.) The evening lowers its grey cold. A garbage truck crashes over the cobblestones and drops a head of cabbage. An urchin in black tatters darts out and nabs it. It's all a black-and-white movie, the same footage every night. Mother Bloor still loves you. The whole country is a black-and-white movie. The image of America is black and white. The shadows are long, as in early morning, or early evening. It's an early Chaplin movie. Chaplin and Paulette Goddard walk off hand-in-hand into the sunset. Vaudeville still exists, the Borscht Circuit still exists, players still clown on baseball diamonds before the big money moves in. FDR's on the radio, laying it out in black and white, a new deal, not yet become the New Deal. "He's a fuckin' genius, if he thinks he can git away with it," Mick said. "A ferkin' genius—I got food on the table—"

In some stadium, Babe Ruth motions at the bleachers, and belts one outa there on the next pitch, his fat ass leisurely circling the bases . . . . Connie Mack cries when he dies—

> *Marie, Marie, the dawn is breaking*
> *Marie, Marie, you'll soon be waking . . .*

April 25, 1945

Admiral:

Sir, the top of the morning to you and the rest of the day to myself.

Enclosed is a letter from Ivan. It was unsealed when it came and that is how I know it is from Ivan and I rubbered at it when I should not have done so, excuse amoi.

All is serene at Plashbourne, we are enjoying our fair modicum of health and happiness. I assume you are off on a long Cruise and it may be quite awhile before we hear from you again. Let us hear, however, when ever you can, as we are always interested in your welfare.

Douglas Lawrence has been drafted, but, I expect the War will be over before he sees Over Seas service.

With a cheerio from us all, I remain, yours for bigger and better wars—

—General *Bisland (ret.)*

My dear A—

How I have thought of you these past few days, far away as you must be by now, and I must tell you of a dream I had last night.

So we were in this room, a large one upstairs somewhere. It was darkish, not colorish. There were lots of bookcases. You were trying to find stuff. I picked up a smallish, 5 or 6 inches, notebook & leafing thru it found that you and Picasso had been having a correspondence about art and that Picasso painted a two-inch line of "work" and then wrote in between the lines. You responded, but only what Picasso did was visible to me.

Then there was a similar notebook, the work of another painter, a landscape painter, beautiful work very traditional work, green trees, again 2-inch lines of painting interwoven with lines of writing to you and no painting of yours visible, not even those astrolabes you used to paint over and over, but then it switches and I see boxes of stuff, and it is clothing and it belonged to your mother Albertine, and you had saved it.

You are in some kind of anguish about this, crying out that Why are you saving this clothing, for what reason when so many in the world are unclothed? This question repeats several times. And I say I know why. It is evidence that she lived. You never really knew her and you need this. It was very emotional. Tears—a few—coming down your face. At one point turning your face head down, leaning against a bookcase. There are letters too, from her, not many, in a fine hand, with some French misspellings, and a photograph of a very tall woman, black-and-white, with large Edwardian style hat, white blouse, Gibson-girl style from waist up, but wearing mid-calf dark skirt and a mid-calf length grey coat. She is turned to the right side.

I feel I know about this clothes-saving business because I have saved some of my mother's things, clothing I associate with her, to make an art piece. Get a clothing dummy, I tell you, and make a piece out of it.

I am aware that you have never mentioned any of this to me in the almost dozen years I've known you! I have to stop now. I was overcome.

Your old friend,

—Sister Helen

The Statue of Liberty
Ellis Island Foundation, Inc.
52 Vanderbilt Avenue
New York, N.Y.

Dear Sir:

We would like to help you in tracing your family's history, however we have no information that can assist you directly. Some handwritten records of immigrants were not always clear as to exact birthplaces.

Sincerely,

—J.G.Seemily

Office of Public Affairs

Oh oh oh I got de Saint Looeey Blues

I got de . . .

The Boys of October:
Rain Delay In Downpour

YANKS DRUM REDS IN 13 INNINGS

THE CURSE OF THE BAMBINO AGAIN
No Joy in Muddy Boston

Hey A—It's been a hellish winter over here, suffering and death and desolation everywhere, no end, no end, fellow man killing fellow man, fellow woman suffering more than fellow man, and the killing goes on in these killing fields, I had never thought to see so many dead and dying in this life, as on these fields, poppy-laden fields . . . fuck it all, I've had enough, I'm copping out, I'm hightailin it outa here, hang my helmet on a trench post along with my gas mask, and I'm off, it's sickening this war of wars, fuck the armaments makers, fuck the totalitarians, fuck the libertarians, fuck the demopubs killing for democracy, fuck the generals, fuck the old guys with their medals on their fat stomachs—Fuck 'em all, fuck 'em all, the long and the short and the tall—

How're they hangin'. Kid?

—Jack the Ripper (that's what they call me in the fuckinplatoon)

"They are murdering all the young men.
For half a century now, every day,
They have hunted them down and killed them . . .
        They are murdering all the young men . . . . '

Dearest One—
                    What are you thinking, thinking,—tell
me, tell me what you're thinking, I never know what you're really
thinking, why can't you tell me ever, I must know, for I love you—
        I try—look on the positive side of things—but my heart is
heavy—
    And I—am I a man or a mouse or a dog—?—I am so dumb—not
stupid but dumb, like an animal.
    I've always been like a young puppy who'll go off with anyone
who ever smiles at him or pets him—
        Most men
                    most men would have left you long ago by now . . . .
        after a whole year of your rejection.
        but still I stick on . . . .
    Don't I get the message? I'm such a dumbskull . . . I don't know
why you're not as sexually starved as I am . . .
No matter—
                —I love you still, ever will—
                                        baisers—xxx—

While we made love
Late that night
In the fall of that year
Among the yellow fallen leaves
Under the linden trees
In Boston Common
In the fall of that year
Where now they are marching again
Waving colored rags of flags again
Under the linden trees
In Boston Common

X

And then the famous Flying Fortress took off bristling with guns and testosterone to make the world safe for peace and capitalism but the birds of peace were nowhere to be found before or after Hiroshima

CAW!
>   *CAW!*
>   *CAW!*

>   that first year after the War
>   at Cape Ann Gloucester
>   on a far shingle long ago—
>   when he put ear to shell
>   of the thundering sea
>   sundering sea
>   seagulls high over
>   calling and cawing
>   back then
>   at Cape Ann Gloucester
>   where poet Olson
>   wrote his own epitaph—
>   "I set out now
>   in a box upon the sea"
>   and poet Creeley found his creel
>   and poet Vincent Ferrini
>   took the wind's clothes
>   and became the conscience of Gloucester
>   The tide-pools gasping
>   the sea's mouth roaring
>   polyphloiboistrous
>   beyond the Ten Pound Light
>   roistering
>   off far islands
>   off *beauport* Gloucester

The seagulls' tattered cries
                    Cats' cries lost
                        reached to us
                              in shredded snatches
                the sea's urge still
                        sea's surge and thunder
                          folded under
The sea still a great door never opened—
        Great ships asunder
                          Clinker-built bottoms
            nets hung with cork
                      hulls heavy with caulking
While still the nor'easter blew
                      still the high tides
                          seethed and swept shoreward
            battered the breakwaters
                    the granite harbors
                              rock villages
          Land's End lashed again
                              in the "sudden fury"
And still the stoned gulls soaring over
                          crying & calling & crying
                blissed out up there
                            in the darkening air
              over the running sea
                            the runing sea
          over dark stone beach under stars . . .

*Far from the sea, far from the sea of Breton fishermen, of
Portuguese fishermen, Italian sailormen—the white clouds scudding
over Lowell, and the white birches, the bare white birches along the
blear night roads, flashing by in darkness And the birch-white face
of a Merrimack madonna shadowed in street light by Merrimack's
shroudy waters—a leaf blown upon sea-wind out of Brittany over
endless oceans—*

There was still a garden
 in the memory of America
There was a nightbird in its memory
There was an *andante cantabile*
in a garden in the memory
of America
In a secret garden
in a private place
a song a melody
a nightsong echoing
in the memory of America
In the sound of a nightbird
outside a Lowell window
In the cry of black kids
in tenement yards at night
In the deep sound
of a woman murmuring
a woman singing broken melody
in a shuttered room
in an old wood house
in Lowell
as the world cracked by
thundering
like a runaway lumber truck
on a steep grade
in Kerouac America
facing a wandering future
without road maps
having long ago come to doubt
Dante's archeology of sin
and other digs in heavenly fields

Yet Ti-Jean Jack
still a heavy believer in Baby Jesus
he with French Canuck tongue
disguised as an American fullback in plaid shirt
crossing and recrossing America
in heaps of cars
Song of the Open Road sung drunken
with Whitman and Jack London and Thomas Wolfe

still echoing through
a Nineteen Thirties America
a Nineteen Forties America
an America long gone now
Except in broken-down dusty old
Greyhound bus stations
in small lost towns
Ti-Jean's vision of America
seen from a speeding car window
the same as Wolfe's lonely sweeping vision
glimpsed from a coach train long ago

'The picture of flashing field, of wood, and hill, stayed in his heart
forever, lost in the dark land . . . . seeing in pale dawn, the phantom
woods, a rutted lane, a cow, a boy, a drab, dull-eyed against a cottage
door . . . . to flash upon the window and be gone.'

A stone, a leaf, an unfound door

And Ti-Jean all his life
(long after he had given up the Road)
never able to go home again—
staggering out of old Lowell bars
to find the "lost lane-end into Heaven"
only to pass out in it
(Look homeward, angel, indeed)
Still writing about feeling like an Indian
neither American nor European
"an exiled American living in America"

I tore up your picture
          when you said goodbye
     I tore up the part
               that once was my heart
  But I put it back together
          I put it back together
               'til death do us part

65

The subjective trying hard
to take back the world
from the objective gorillas of the world
In two hundred years of freedom
they had invented
the permanent alienation of the subjective
Almost every truly creative being
alienated and expatriated
in his own country
in Middle America or San Francisco
The short-haired hard heads
who still ruled everything
stood like menhirs
over the dark land
The alienated generations
lived out their expatriate visions
here and everywhere
The old generations lived them out
Lived out the bohemian myth in Greenwich Villages
Lived out the Hemingway myth
as the sun also rose (and set)
on the Dôme in Paris
or with the bulls at Pamplona
Lived out the Henry Miller myth
in the *Tropics* of Paris
And the great Greek dream
of *The Colossus of Maroussi*
And the tropic dream of Gauguin
And the D.H. Lawrence myth
in *The Plumed Serpent*
in Mexico Lake Chapala
And the Malcolm Lowry myth
Under the Volcano at Cuernavaca
And then the saga of On the Road
And Bob Dylan blowing in the wind
How many roads must a man walk down
How many Neal Cassadys on lost railroad tracks
How many replicas of Woody Guthrie with cracked guitar

How many photocopies of long-haired Joan
How many Ginsberg facsimiles and carbon-copy Keseys
wandering the streets of America
in old tennis shoes and backpacks
or driving beat-up buses
with destination-signs reading *FURTHER*
How many Buddhist Catholics how many cantors
chanting the Great Paramita Sutra
on the Lower East Side
How many *Whole Earth Catalogs*
lost in outhouses in New Mexico communes—

      The lonely and isolate satyrs

                                   are everywhere

    Horsemen and bikers charge
        over the landscape westward
            their penises raised like lances

Americus Maximus or Minimus,
standing on the corner
of Love and Hate Streets
In the country of the young
hitchhiking westward ever
thumb extended
A train far-off
hooting its loneliness
in darks of night

OUTMODED CAPITALISM
THREATENS HUMANITY
WITH MULTIPLE PERILS

—-Pathogenic Industrial Output —-

We were sailing along on moonlight bay
You could hear the voices ringing
You could hear them singing . . .

My very dearest A—Shall I call you? Just send me a card or write me a real letter. Let me know the real things—Are you happy? Do you think about me ever?—-about the two of us? Will we ever be together? . . . I am still here—-You know where I am—carpe diem, carpe noctem! *"But to you, without my moving, without seeing you, distant you, Go my blood and my kisses"*

—Your Annie

So that's the way it always is and the fire and the rose are one and always the same scene and always the same subject right from the beginning like in the Bible or *The Sun Also Rises* which begins Robert Cohn was once middleweight boxing champion of his class but later we lost our balls there's the same old theme and scene again with all the citizens and all the characters all working up to it right from the first and it looks like all they ever think of is doing IT and it doesn't matter much with whom half the time but the other half it matters more than anything O the sweet love fevers yes and there's always complications like maybe she has no eyes for him or him no eyes for her or her no eyes for her or him no eyes for him or something or other stands in the way like his mother or her father or someone like that but they go right on trying to get IT all the time like in Shakespeare or Proust and his Odette and their "cattleyas" and on and on And everyone struggling toward each other or after each other like those marble maidens on that Grecian Urn or on any market street or merry-go-round around and around they go all hunting "love" and half the hungry time not even knowing just what is really eating them like Robin in her *Nightwood* streets although it isn't quite as simple as all that as if all she really needed was a good five-cent cigar oh no and those who have not hunted will not recognize the hunting poise and then the hawks that hover where the heart is hid and the hungry horses crying and the stone angels and heaven and hell and Yerma yearning with her blind breasts under her dress and then Christopher Columbus sailing off in search and Rudolph

Valentino and Juliet and Romeo and John Barrymore and Anna Livia and Abie's Irish Rose and so Goodnight Sweet Prince all over again with everyone and everybody laughing and crying along wherever night and day winter and summer spring and tomorrow like Anna Karenina lost in the snow and the cry of hunters in a great wood and the soldiers coming and Freud and Ulysses always on their hungry travels after the same hot grail like King Arthur and his nighttime knights and everybody wondering where and how it will all end like in the movies or in some nightmaze novel yes as in a nightmaze Yes I said Yes I will and he called me his Andalusian Rose and I said Yes his heart was going like mad And that's the way *Ulysses* ends as everything always ends when that hunting cock of flesh at last cries out and has his glory moment God and then comes tumbling down the sound of axes in the wood and the trees falling and down it goes the sweet cock's sword so wilting in the fair flesh fields away alone at last and loved and lost and found upon a riverbank along a riverrun right where it all began and so begins again—

XI

Greater Manhattan!
Ville Tentaculaire!
Fourmillante cité Humanité en masse

On upper Fifth Avenue by Grand Army Plaza
the dignified doorman
with the scrambled eggs on his visor
(looking like General MacArthur
about to wade ashore)
opens the door

    Winter's back is broken
        The squirrels are out in Central Park
            A hansom cab through the park
             an old white horse pulling
                  the old open carriage
                       clop-clop
          Cabby on the seat
               in his high hat
                    dead asleep
        The horse
            slows to a stop at the curb
       The cabby awakes
             Where away?
        Anywhere!
            cry the two together
               wrapped in each other
    Spring about to happen
        A flight of dirty doves
            takes off from the still-bare trees
      The eternal coachman
            moves his reins
   Clop-clop goes the horse
         Kiss-kiss cry the birds
             in a song without words

And retired ballerinas on winter afternoons walking their dogs in Central Park West (or their cats on leashes—the cats themselves old highwire artists) The ballerinas leap and pirouette through Columbus Circle while winos on park benches (laid back like drunken Godunovs) hear the taxis trumpet together like horsemen of the apocalypse in the dusk of the gods It is the final witching hour when swains are full of swan songs And all return through the dark dusk to their bright cells in glass highrises or sit down to oval cigarettes and cakes in the Russian Tea Room or climb four flights to back rooms in West Side brownstones where faded playbill photos fall peeling from their frames like last year's autumn leaves

My dear, my dear . . . . In spite of all—through it all—I loved you and loved you—Now, still, I love you—even though it can no longer be—even as I know—even as I know—that the door we never opened (into a rose garden!) now we can never open—I don't know what I'm ever going to do—Sometimes—sometimes I feel like the Young Werther—sometimes I think I'll— Oh I must stop now—

Recently regilded
General Sherman marches bravely
on his great grey stallion
through Central Park South
into Grand Army Plaza
led by a Delacroix lady liberty
(pressed into service by the military)
and carrying an extra large olive branch
while from her back sprout
huge gelt wings
and on the stone ground
next to the horse's left leg
lies a torn branch
of some great old evergreen
as if in this wood
the General had beheld
the much-touted
Golden Bough of antiquity

but had indeed cast it aside
having greater money-trees in mind
headed downtown
where the big gelt is dealt

Those stone canyons again
the heartless canyons . . .
hard arteries in the heart of the beast
Ashcans and unobtainable dollars!
The fever of savage city life
still grips the streets
Hunger and loneliness
or a full stomach and loneliness
day after day
night after endless night
The muddled masses
huddled in shelters

In the Public Library
West 53rd Street
the guards go 'round
waking the homeless sleeping on books
In the Men's Room
graffito says
> *Cathlic Church*
> *Mudered Muther*

In Rockefeller Center
deep in the bowels of the Time-Life building
a scurvy crew of low-pay WWII vets
(disgruntled front-line grunts and below-decks Hairy Apes)
manned the mailroom of Time, Inc.
intent on wreaking havoc
on the capitalist empire
gleefully mis-sorting its mail
in surrealist configurations
much to the consternation of top-floor brass
on their way to three-hour lunches

Way downtown on Seventh Avenue
in the window of a shop called
Dresses for Miss
a bunch of inflated bras
with promise of pneumatic bliss

Way downtown
in the Athens Grill & Bar
at the counter they are
watching the ponies at Pimlico
at Churchill Downs
at the Elysian Fields
the Greek proprietor (or his brother)
brings the menu
with a strong recommendation to eat
the Special Greek Spinach Pie
The bangtails break from the gate
They're off and running
"Some hosses!" goes the counterman
like he's watching
the horses of Achilles
And in prances
a blond bimbo with beautiful bumpers
with a guy in a tux in tow
and they flop down in a back booth
carrying on real lovey-dovey
And two old dames
with accents and attitudes
and lotsa lipstick
come in singly and take booths and order
They're fast on the uptake
and give the boss a lotta lip
They come to drink
to eat and drink
and watch the ponies on tv
their husbands long gone
What else they got to do?
This is their life
Lower East Side

The ponies and the Greek proprietor
and the Greek-Italian dinners
and the tv behind the bar
The ponies are coming round the bend
Big Boy in Charge
Lady Be Mine
Seabiscuit
Mutineer
Hot Stud
Empire Builder
Sugar Daddy
They're coming down the stretch
One widow got the hots for the counterman
the boss or his brother
She wishes she could
come first in his race
To Place or To Show won't do
She needs to ride him
into the Winner's Circle
and wrap her arms or legs around him
like a wreath
and trot him home with her
in the final race
But
like I said
the odds ain't good—

              I am your siren singer
              I have a voice like an angel
              a husky voice a musky voice
              in a piano bar at One Fifth Avenue

              Oh I am your siren singer
              I am your angel of light
              your lady of light
              I am your heart breaker
              Your ball breaker
              And I know you love me baby
              love me love me

Way down in Tompkins Square
a dirty crescent moon
high over the bare old trees
standing silent
The trees in there always
where they hide the shivs
waiting for you in the dark
in the dense dark—
Bare ruined choirs!

Way east of Tompkins a war zone
Dresden West with embellishments
New World Symphony with Sirens

Streetlights shot out Garbage fires in smoking lots Spectral tenements
Burned-out box factories Abandoned missions Tarpaper shelters
Ashcan fires and shit Streetcorner deals and death Fucking on fire-
escapes Narco Nirvanas . . .

*"Astride of a grave, the light gleams for an instant, then it's night
once more."*

Whereas a gaggle of beat upstart crows
rose over the rooftops of tenement boneyards
intent on making out
(in bed with poetry)
while up at Columbia
lady critics and gent professors
and various *New Yorker*ish poetasters
on the Times Square Shuttle
between the *Times Book Review* and the Algonquin
moaned about these poetic pederasts
who took to the wildest side of the road
waving genitals and manuscripts
tuning their holy unholy voices
to a wide-open society
that didn't yet exist
And so jump-started

the stalled merry-go-round of American ecstasy
left along East River's echoing shores
after old Walt stepped off Brooklyn Ferry
into the heart of America

And the New York Abstract Expressionists
with their primal nonobjective images
destroying the fine arts tradition
of their Euro fathers
mirroring in the shattered light
of their action paint
"the shattering of civilization itself"
(as mouthed in museum glosses
which most of the painters themselves
never thought of
but later exclaimed "Right on!"
on their way to the bank)

Two Hearts Ripped out of City

TEAMS SOLD OUT!

NY GIANTS TO FRISCO
BROOKLYN DODGERS TO L.A.

DEM BUMS IS GONE
Dark Day in Brooklyn

Casey Stengel: "It stinks!"
Yogi Berra: "It's oveh!"

A Death in the Family:
Black Banners on Ebbetts Field

FUNERAL PARADE MARKS END OF ERA

XII

Who are we now, who are we ever—
Skin books Parchment bodies Libraries of the living
Gilt almanachs of the very rich
Encylopedias of little people
Jacks and Queens of Hearts
face-up on maps of America
the face-cards of some new consciousness
(and consciousness itself perhaps a disaster)
born of the vortex of the Renaissance
and the vortex of the Twentieth century—
their fate to face
the paroxysm of the Twenty-first

(Though some like Ezra Pound
turned their backs on America
and took ship for the last time
back to the crenelated camembert
of olde Europa
on the SS *Cristòforo Colombo*—
it too having reversed course)

But the masses pressed on
A crowd flowed over Brooklyn Bridge
and took a taxi West
Took a train West
Took a plane West
with ten million others
Tilting the continent up
like a huge scale

    I never thought of where I come from
                        until I left it behind . . .

Uprooted by war
hundreds of thousands of loose people

like a tidal wave
And the wave sweeps westward
Prairie schooners into Pullmans
their bright saloons sheeted in oblivion
bodies nested in them
hurtled through the night
Inscrutable

"How fur ye goin'?"

"I dunno . . . Pretty far—"

Rock Revolution & Sexual Revolution Allow
Easy Access to Sex
Girlie Mags Slump
"No Need for Photos" Says Critic

PRESIDENT ASSASSINATED!
JFK GUNNED DOWN IN DALLAS!

Plot Suspected
FBI & CIA Involved

NATIONAL TRAUMA

"WE KNOW
HIS NAME WRITTEN
IN THE BLACK CAPITALS
  OF HIS DEATH,
  AND THE MOURNERS
  STANDING IN THE RAIN,
  AND THE LEAVES
  FALLING . . . . "

We are poor little lambs who have lost their way
We are poor little sheep—

And we tune to a raga on the stereo
and turn on Death TV without its sound
Outside the plums are growing in a tree
"The force that through the green fuse drives the flower"
drives Death TV
And they lower the body soundlessly
into a huge plane in Dallas
marked United States of America
and soundlessly the "United States of America"
takes off and wings away with that body
through its sky full of shit and death
as it wings soundlessly
from that fucked-up city
whose name we'd rather not remember
Inside the plane a wife lies soundlessly
against the coffin
Engine whines as sitar sings outrageously
as the "United States of America"
flies on sightlessly
through the swift fierce years
with the dead weight of the Body
that they keep flying from Dallas
that they keep flying
from Los Angeles
And the plane lands
without folding its wings
its shadow in mourning for itself

And then they are driving the Body
up Fifth Avenue
past a million people in line
The cortege passes soundlessly
"Goodbye! Goodbye!" some people cry
And they lift the body of the United States of America
and carry it into a cathedral
singing Hallelujah He Shall Live Forever and Ever
And the Body moves again
Fifty-seven black sedans after it
There are people with roses behind the barricades
in bargain-basement dresses
And they put that Body in a long train
And the funeral train the silver train starts up again
Soundlessly
at a dead speed
over the hot land
an armed helicopter over it
They are clearing the tracks ahead of assassins
The tracks are lined with bare faces
A high school band in New Jersey plays
the "Battle Hymn of the Republic"
They have shot it down again
They have shot him down again
and will shoot him down again
and take him on a train
and lower him again
into a grave in Washington
Day and night journeys the coffin
through the dark land
too dark now to see the dark faces
People with roses behind the barricades

"Moloch! Solitude! Filth! Ugliness! Ashcans and unob-
tainable dollars! Children screaming under the
stairways! Boys sobbing in the armies! Old men
weeping in the parks!"

Cityfull passing away . . . houses . . . streets . . . miles of pavements
. . . Pyramids in sand No one is anything . . . .

"Visions! omens! hallucinations! miracles! ecstasies!
gone down the American river!
Dreams! adorations! illuminations! religions! The whole
boatload of sensitive bullshit!"

Yet still endless the splendid life of the world

Endless its lovely living and
breathing its lovely sentient beings seeing and hearing
feeling and thinking laughing and dancing sighing and
crying through endless afternoons endless nights
drinking and doping talking and singing in autumn
capitals and sleep unraveling the knitted sleeves of
care the labyrinths of thought the labyrêves of love
the coils of longing myriad endgames of the unname-
able Endless the heavens on fire endless universe
spun out World upon a mushroom pyre Endless the
fire that breathes in us Tattooed fire-eaters dancing in
plazas swallowing flaming gasoline air Brave the beat-
ing heart of flaming life its beating and pulsings and
flame-outs Endless the open fields of the senses the
smell of lust and love the calling and calling of cats in
heat their scent of must of musk No end to the making
of love to the sound of bedsprings creaking to the

moan of lovers making it heard through the wall at night moans of the last lost climax the sound of jukebox jumping the flow of jass and gyzm jived in Paradiso Endless *l'homme revolté* in the anonymous face of death in the tracks of the monster State his anarchist visions his alienation his alienated poetry Gadfly of the state Bearer of Eros his automatic writings and scrawlings *poèmes dictés* by the Unknown and telephone calls to ends of earth The waiting of lovers on station platforms the cawing of crows the myriad churning of crickets the running seas the crying waters rising and falling on far shingles the lapping of tides in the Ides of autumn salt kiss of creation No end to the sea bells tolling beyond the dykes the calling of bells in empty churches and towers of time No end to the calamitous enunciation of hairy holy man Endless the ever-unwinding watchspring heart of the world shimmering in time shining through space No end to the birthing of babies where love or lust has lain No end to the sweet birth of consciousness to the bitter deaths of it in vain No end no end to the withering of fur and fruit and flesh so passing fair and the neon mermaids singing each to each somewhere The fires of youth the embers of age the rage of the poet born again No end no end to the muted dance of molecules All is transmuted All is muted and all cries out again again Endless the wars of good and evil the flips of fate the trips of hate nukes and faults all failing-safe in chain reactions of the final flash while the White Bicycles of protest still circle round it For there

will be an end to the dogfaced gods in wingtip shoes in
Gucci slippers in Texas boots and tin hats in bunkers
pressing buttons For there are hopeful choices still to
be chosen the dark minds lighted in Stonewall bars
the green giants of chance the fishhooks of hope in the
sloughs of despond the hills in the distance the birds
in the bush the hidden streams of light and unheard
melodies the sessions of sweet silent thought stately
pleasure domes decreed and the happy deaths of the
heart every day the cocks of clay the feet in running
shoes upon the quay And there is no end no end to the
doors of perception still to be opened and the jet
streams of light in the upper air of the spirit of man in
the outer space inside us

     Shining! Transcendent!

Into the crystal night of time

    In the endless silence of the soul

In the long loud tale of man

     In his endless sound and fury

signifying everything

  The dancing continues

    There is a sound of revelry by night

NOTES

I
p. 1: "To summarize the past . . ."—T.S. Eliot, *Selected Essays*

p. 1: "felt life"—Hugh Kenner, *The Pound Era*

p. 2: "Wrought from the dark in his mother long ago"—A variation on Bertolt Brecht's "Brought from the dark by my mother long ago."

p. 3: "A small-scale exhibition"—Sadegh Hedayat, *The Owl*

p. 3: "Demon or bird!"—Walt Whitman, *Leaves of Grass*

p. 3: "Men Seeking Women"—Classified ad in the *San Francisco Bay Guardian*

II
p. 6: "Beginning with Sunday at the beach"—William Carlos Williams, *Paterson*

p. 6: "Time the wisest of things . . . "—Attributed to Thales

p. 6: "Time . . . An arrow flying both ways . . ."—*Scientific American*, 1970s

p. 7: "the thinkpad . . ."—Lord Buckley, *Hiparama of the Classics*

III
p. 9: "the great crystal ball"—Ezra Pound, Canto CXVI

p. 9: "Crystal Palace"—Dostoevsky, *Notes from Underground*

p.10: "who obeys the figures of the present dance"—Charles Olson, *Maximus*

p.11: "in this foul country . . ."—*Ibid.* The relevant context reads:
". . . how many waves
of hell and death and
dirt and shit
meaningless waves of hurt and punished lives shall America
be nothing but the story of
not all her successes
—I have been—Leroy has been
as we genetic failures are
successes, here
it isn't interesting
Yankees—Europeans—Chinese

what is the heart, turning

beating itself out leftward

in hell to know heaven . . . ."

p. 11: "all you finger-poppin daddies . . ."—Lord Buckley, *op. cit.*

p. 11: "gifted with 'giftlessness'"—Dostoevsky, *op. cit.*, and Vladimir Nabokov, *The Gift*

IV

p. 19: "And then went down to the ship . . ."—Pound, Canto I (after Homer)

p. 19: "What ships what shores . . ."—Cf. T.S. Eliot, "Marina"

p. 19: "What songs the sirens sang . . ."—Dudley Fitts, *Poems*

p. 19: "So suddenly out of its stale and drowsy lair . . ."—Whitman, *op. cit.*

p. 20: "Johan Padan . . ."—Dario Fo, *A la descoverta de la Americhe*

p. 21: "Old men carrying their fathers . . ."—Malcolm Lowry, *Under the Volcano*

p. 21: "'Tierra y Libertad!' cried an army of Indians . . ."—B. Traven, *General from the Jungle*

p. 22: "the *Mayflower* had landed . . ."—Howard Zinn, *A People's History of the United States*

p. 22: "Boston's Tea Party . . ."—Thom Hartmann, *Unequal Protection: The Rise of Corporate Dominance and the Theft of Human Rights*

p. 22: "a man of no fortune . . ."—Pound, Canto I

p. 23: "Twain . . . the Lincoln of our lit[erature]"—William Dean Howells

V

p. 24: "To write a Republic . . . in Blueberry America"—Robert Creeley, Foreword to *Collected Poems of Charles Olson*

p. 24: "For who controls the present . . ."—George Orwell, *1984*

p. 25: "Whereas the people wrote their own history . . . to wit"—The next seventeen lines are taken verbatim from the table of contents of Zinn, *op. cit.*

p. 27: "TELL HOW THEY FLEW!"—*The Smithsonian*, April 2003

p. 27: "The past a mess of blood and sorrow"—Langston Hughes, *Poems*

p. 28: "shaking the wings 'of his exultant youth'"—James Joyce, *A Portrait of the Artist as a Young Man*

p. 28: "Was there not one moment in time . . ."—Sadegh Hedayat, *op. cit.*

VI

VII

hardier for that repression—waiting terribly to break forth, revenge-
ful—the execution of the king and queen—the tempest of massacres
and blood. Yet who can wonder?"

p. 38: *"La vida es sueño"*—Calderón de la Barca

p. 39: "Faÿ"—Bernard Faÿ, a collaborator with the Nazis and a fine friend
of Gertrude Stein. Cf. Janet Malcolm, "Gertrude Stein's War," *The
New Yorker*, June 2, 2003

p. 39: "Oh I'm a Yankee Doodle dandy . . ."—George M. Cohan

p. 39: "The spell of arms and voices . . ."—James Joyce, *op. cit.*

p. 39: Re Hepburn—Cf. Claudia Roth Pierpont, "Born for the Part," *The
New Yorker*, July 14 and 21, 2003

p. 40: ". . . I am not familiar with the exact constitution of the Tarot pack
of cards . . ."—T.S. Eliot, "Notes on 'The Waste Land'"

p. 40: *"The last time I saw Paris . . ."*—Oscar Hammerstein, 1940. Cf. Also
Eliott Paul.

p. 40: ". . . sous le pont Mirabeau . . ."—Guillaume Apollinaire, *Alcools*

p. 40: *"Au revoir, les enfants . . ."*—From the Louis Malle film of that name

p. 40: "the parody of *Le Paradis Artificiel* . . ."—Pound, *op. cit.*

p. 41: *"Lilli Marlene . . ."*—Broadcast to American troops by Nazi radio
during the Second World War.

p. 41: *"Marie, Marie, hold on tight . . ."*—T.S. Eliot, "The Burial of the
Dead"

p. 41: *"Quand on est dans la merde . . ."*—Samuel Beckett

p. 42: "Rappelle-toi Barbara . . ."—Jacques Prévert, *Paroles*

VIII

p. 43: "A hopefulness without frontiers . . ."—John Berger in *Harper's
Magazine*, March 2003

p. 44: "lives haunted by a Georgia slattern . . ."—Wolfe, *op. cit.*

p. 45: *"Yes, we have no bananas"*—The words of this song were said to have
been uttered by a Long Island fruit peddler."—James S. Fuld, *op.
cit.*

p. 47: "America hangs in midair . . ."—Laura Hillenbrand, *Seabiscuit: An
American Legend*

p. 49: "Good evening, Mr. & Mrs. North and South America . . ."—Walter
Winchell's introduction to his daily radio show.

p. 51: *"Oh if I had the wings of an angel"*—Guy Massey, "The Prisoner's
Song," 1924

p. 51: "If it had not been for these thing . . ."—Transcribed from the words of Bartolomeo Vanzetti at his trial. The typography used here poorly imitates Ben Shahn's graphic rendering in his serigraph, *The Passion of Sacco and Vanzetti.*

p. 52: "Twenty or thirty years ago, when all the birds began to sing . . ." First sentence in Alfred Kazin, *On Native Grounds*

p. 52: "A Tate-worm . . ."—Attributed to Kenneth Rexroth

p. 52: *"To the tables down at Mory's . . ."*—"The Whiffenpoof Song" at Yale

p. 53: *"Come on and hear . . . Alexander's Ragtime Band . . ."*—Irving Berlin, 1911

IX

p. 57: "HERE DOWN ON DARK EARTH / Before we all go to Heaven . . ." —Jack Kerouac, "Blues"

p. 57: *"And thus did he see first the dark land"*—Thomas Wolfe, *op. cit.*

p. 61: *"They are murdering all the young men . . ."*—Kenneth Rexroth, "Thou Shalt Not Kill"

X

p. 65: "The picture of flashing field..."—Wolfe, *op. cit.*

p. 65: *"A stone, a leaf, an unfound door"*—*Ibid.*

p. 65: "lost lane-end into Heaven"—*Ibid.*

p. 67: *"The lonely and isolate satyrs"*—Charles Olson, *Maximus*

p. 68: *"But to you, without my moving, without seeing you . . ."*—Pablo Neruda, "Always"

XI

p. 70: *"Ville tentaculaire!"*—Cf. Emile Verhaeren, *Les villes tentaculaires,* and Lawrence Ferlinghetti, *La cité, symbole dans la poésie moderne* (doctoral thesis, University of Paris)

p. 71: *"the door we never opened (into a rose garden!) . . ."*—A variation of lines in Eliot, "Burnt Norton"

p. 72: *"Ashcans and unobtainable dollars!"*—Allen Ginsberg, *Howl*

p. 75: *"Astride of a grave . . ."*—Samuel Beckett

XII

p. 77: "and consciousness itself perhaps a disaster"—Dostoevsky, *op. cit.*

p. 78: "'How fur ye goin?' 'I dunno . . . Pretty far.'"—What the truck driver said at the end of Dos Passos, *Manhattan Transfer*

p. 78: "WE KNOW HIS NAME . . ."—The typography and line-breaks here are based on Ben Shahn's lettering of Wendell Berry's poem in Shahn's *November Twenty-Six Nineteen Hundred Sixty-Three*

p. 81: *"Moloch! Solitude! . . ."*—Ginsberg, *op. cit.*

p. 81: *"Cityfull passing away . . ."*—James Joyce, *Finnegans Wake*

p. 81: *"Visions! Omens! . . ."*—Ginsberg, *op. cit.*

p. 83: *"There is a sound of revelry by night"*—George Noel Gordon, Lord Byron, *Childe Harold's Pilgrimage*, Canto III (Before the Battle of Waterloo)